Etiquettes
and
Manners
Plain
and
Simple

Etiquettes
and
Manners

Plain
and
Simple

Successful Tips for
Successful People:
Best Practices for
Boys, Girls, *and* Future Leaders

Jackie F. Whitehead, EdD

n ARCHWAY
PUBLISHING

Archway Publishing books may be ordered through booksellers or by contacting:

Archway Publishing
1663 Liberty Drive
Bloomington, IN 47403
www.archwaypublishing.com
1 (888) 242-5904

Because of the dynamic nature of the Internet, any web addresses or
links contained in this book may have changed since publication and
may no longer be valid. The views expressed in this work are solely those
of the author and do not necessarily reflect the views of the publisher,
and the publisher hereby disclaims any responsibility for them.

Any people depicted in stock imagery provided by Getty Images are
models, and such images are being used for illustrative purposes only.
Certain stock imagery © Getty Images.

This book is a work of non-fiction. Unless otherwise noted, the author
and the publisher make no explicit guarantees as to the accuracy of
the information contained in this book and in some cases, names of
people and places have been altered to protect their privacy.

ISBN: 978-1-4808-7511-1 (sc)
ISBN: 978-1-4808-7512-8 (hc)
ISBN: 978-1-4808-7510-4 (e)

Library of Congress Control Number: 2019904842

Print information available on the last page.

Archway Publishing rev. date: 4/30/2019

Contents

Dedications

I dedicate this book to my daughters, Jane and Jill. They have listened and improved on etiquettes and manners taught them through well-known traditions by way of our family time together and our interactions within real-world scenarios. Many of the standards and tips in this book helped them successfully engage in mature social interactions, travel, business, academics, and everyday life communications. These valued concepts continue to reflect on them successfully in leadership roles and in their personal professionalism. Happily, they have become highly effective communicative role models with a solid etiquette repertoire.

Next, I dedicate my work to my husband, Jimmy. He has supported all of my many ventures, projects, and creative ideas. And to my mother, Alice, who was always there to help me develop my character as I grew up.

Lastly, I dedicate parts of my book to my friend Donna.

Through the years, we made it our mission in life to help young girls and boys gain and develop hands-on etiquette skills and use them as lifelong compasses toward good manners, helping them build strong foundations through the use of etiquettes for keys to success.

Preface

Luck is fickle and by no means reliable. Do not count on luck to get you anywhere. Education is a trustworthy foundation for building character and tools for recognition. Educating one's self should be a lifelong process. Whether tapping into or tweaking general common sense, learning by way of real-world, hands-on experiences, or by taking structured academics, you can be assured that highly sought wisdom is gained by fusing all the above in your path of lifelong learning. Confidence comes with knowledge; success comes with preparation. Which brings to mind an important notion to ponder and considered over all else. This wisdom I speak of has been relayed throughout the ages and sermonized in a variety of ways. To the point, it is believed the philosopher Aristophanes once wrote, and I roughly translate the concept as I heard it, "Youth ages, immaturity is outgrown, ignorance can be educated, and drunkenness sobered, but stupid lasts forever." Whether he said it or not, the point is to not be one of the "stupid" people. Be a seeker of wisdom, confidence, and success. The tips in this book can help you succeed with all three ideals. It all starts with etiquettes and manners, plain and simple.

Introduction

You have probably heard the old proverb, "Clothes make a man (or women)." To be more accurate, we could add that it should also be said that following basic etiquettes and manners are key ingredients for a successful life, subsequent to whether that life is social, academic, or professional. Etiquettes and manners separate and elevate us within creation. These basic learned attributes are linked to communicative success and perceptions of self-worth. Ultimately, they help us develop as social capital within our personal worlds. And although we sometimes do not want to admit it, nothing feels better than to have value in the eyes of others.

It is important to note that first impressions only come around once. Do not waste your moments in time. Be prepared when they come. Developing mature core etiquettes and manners do not become part of one's self overnight. They are attributes in progress. Time spent is well worth your while for strong personal growth. It is never too late to be what you want to be. And it is never too late to start developing successful character traits so you can be perceived well by others. You never know when that spotlight will shine on you. Be ready.

If you have not done so already, start thinking of etiquettes and manners as powerful tools for advancement in all areas of life, if for no other reason than to give and gain respect of other human beings. All of which, when you think of it, are strong concepts that separate humans from animals. In short, etiquettes and manners are behavioral ideals that tell us how to behave when we interact with other people. In turn, they help us succeed routinely and/or conquer difficult scenarios. These learned behaviors make people like, respect, and consider us more; consequently, making us and others more at ease while communicating in positive ways. Success!

Etiquettes and manners are easy to learn, and they basically never change. Therefore, once learned in youth, these same principles can be enhanced and built upon as adults. Well-played etiquettes and manners can help you stand out in the crowd. So do not just read this book once; use it as a lifelong reference. Remember, it never hurts to refresh your etiquette knowledge and skills from time to time. This book helps you now and in your future. Until you have the rules of etiquette down pat, refer to the book before you go out to dinner, to a meeting, or to a party, so you will remember just how to act and make a great first impression every time.

Chapter 1

Etiquette versus Manners: The Importance of Both

Good manners are simply polite, kind ways to behave with others. Manners are acceptable social conduct and norms of a specific society, period, or group that seldom change. They are easy to learn. It is important to learn good manners from your elders particularly and/or from those who set the standards for particular social customs; specifically, from those who teach what is acceptable in your specific social environment. Manners are a way of treating someone, most often using positive moral content or demeanors and conducted by and between people. They are sometimes considered mature "social graces." Good manners are an example of your character and maturity, a sample of your respect for yourself and others. A person's outward bearing or charming manners offer him or her an air of distinction in the environments where the individual mingles. Manners are not just for formal times or events. They are required on a daily basis to communicate and function as civil human beings.

Etiquettes, on the other hand, are the sets of practices, or actions, of manner methods. They are the standards of specific practices prescribed by social conventions or by authorities. They are the ways of doing something or how something happens. Etiquettes are socially correct practices, styles, or methods of execution. They are evidence of prevailing customs. Furthermore, etiquettes are conventional physical requirements for proper social behaviors in matters of ceremonies or events. In short, etiquettes are codes of ethical behaviors among members of detailed professions or specific groups. Translating manners into etiquettes helps one fit into society more easily, lending a hand to acceptance, effective communication, and getting along with others.

Notes

_____

_____

_____

_____

_____

_____

_____

_____

_____

_____

_____

_____

_____

_____

_____

Chapter 2

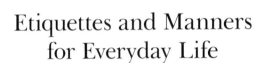

Etiquettes and Manners for Everyday Life

Listening and contributing to a conversation are major parts of the fine art of useful communication. Having etiquette and showing manners during social, business, or academic conversations are important to your success in life as a human being in general, and to your success in your career path specifically. To communicate properly, it is very important to look someone in the eyes when carrying on a conversation. This helps make sure the conversation has your and the other person's full attention. When you give your full attention to a conversation—whether talking or listening—makes it less likely you'll give or receive bad communication or miscommunication. When bad communication or miscommunication occurs, many problems in understanding the purpose or importance of a conversation can result. Also, not listening fully during a conversation can bring about wrong impressions for all communicators involved.

When you are involved in a conversation, you are basically in a contract with the others involved in the information exchange. You either communicate or receive information in a positive or negative manner. Successful people communicate and receive information in a positive way. For example, maintaining positive eye contact can help keep the attention of those you are talking with. It almost forces one to give the conversation your full attention, making it an act of true communication. Misunderstandings are less likely. And, if someone has hearing difficulties, looking at the person face-to-face as you communicate is just polite. Besides, yelling or speaking loudly at them does not necessarily help them hear you. Find the balance.

Think of responding to others using positive cues. It is said that positivity breeds positivity, and negativity breeds negativity. For example, instead of saying, "I'm sorry I missed the meeting," say, "Thank you for understanding my absence from the meeting." Or, instead of, "I'm sorry I didn't contribute to the group," say, "I'm glad the group managed well without me." It is best to carry on conversations in positive ways. In doing so, you come off as a positive person. People like positive people. Positive people get more done.

Gum Is Not Your Friend

When in a group or just with a friend, if not done properly, chewing gum can be rude. If you chew gum, as with food, keep your mouth closed! Open mouth chewing, popping, and/or loud smacking are not polite. Also important to remember is when you are finished chewing your gum, place it in a trash can. Never spit your gum out on the ground or place under a seat, table, or arm of a chair. And absolutely do not swallow it.

Taking, Posting, or Tagging Photos on Social Media

It is important to get permission from others before you take, post, or tag them in a group or individual photo and place it on social media. This is true especially of unflattering photos. It is also important to be careful of the photos you post of yourself. Make sure all photos you post are in good taste. It is one thing to post fun photos but entirely something else to post ones in bad taste. Remember, what you post is always and forever on the internet.

Gossiping and Telling Secrets

It is not polite to gossip. Gossiping or spreading gossip is a sign of having poor manners and inadequate character. It is rude to tell secrets in front of others. If you have something to say to someone in particular, wait until you are alone with the person to share your thoughts privately.

Neither behavior leads to success. If you cannot say it in a group, it does not need to be said. You do not want to contribute to giving out false information or be part of a slander campaign.

Notes

Chapter 3

Phones and Texting

Nothing is worse than being with someone who cannot take a break from his or her phone to share a meal, moment, event, or outing with others. Moreover, in a small-group scenario, nothing is as rude as having one totally engaged with a phone and not the group. Doing so gives the impression that the phone—or whoever is on the other end of the call or text—is much more important than you or your group. Conversation is a two-way street of focused listening and vocal reaction. You must contribute to the conversation in both ways to have positive and productive interactions with others.

First, no one wants to hear your phone conversation or be disrupted by it. And, second, no one likes to feel less important or ignored for someone else's social text or phone call. Being on the phone or another device makes those at a social gathering feel like their time is not as important as yours. Furthermore, people on the phone tend to become distracted by their device instead of being engaged with the group or social situation. They fail as effective and productive conversationalists. Therefore, it is best to silence or store your device if possible when socializing or involved in professional conversation.

Successful people know best practices when participating in social or business conversations. Phones and similar devices are big distractions to successful face-to-face communication. In business, it is more professional to conscientiously limit all distractions while carrying on business conversations, meetings, luncheons, and other gatherings. It could make the difference between successful or lost negotiations.

Face-to-face interactions are always best understood because they are vocal and direct. They are more personal. It is important to remember that texting can be and often is misinterpreted. Often, it is difficult for text communication to reflect context, deeper meanings, and emotions. Therefore, it is probable that texting will at some point break down successful communication. It can develop serious problems, whether with the person you are texting or by causing an issue with the person or people you are with physically. Hence, it is wise to store your device while part of professional situations.

On a more casual level, if it is not practical to temporarily store your device, social groups have begun the practice of stacking their phones all together in the center of the table to show their commitment to the gathering and giving their full attention to each other. Even so, you obliviously cannot ignore an incoming call or text during one-on-one or small-group social gatherings, but you can respond to it with a polite, "decline to engage," or an "auto message" that reflects your pause to answer incoming phone calls or texts. If someone really needs to speak with you, the person will leave a message or call again later. If you must answer the call or text, it is always best to answer quickly and explain that you are in a situation where you cannot talk or text at the moment. Thus, handling the situation while not alienating or reducing the importance of the caller or texter. It is polite to promise to return the call or text at a more appropriate time in the near future; and do so.

Of course, emergency situations override this procedure. In case of an emergency call or text, you should excuse yourself from the gathering or person you are with to take the call or respond to the text. If necessary, excuse yourself from the group or situation entirely and move away. Make sure to speak softly so as not to disrupt the others' socialization.

All of these etiquettes are perhaps most important when in an elegant restaurant, café, meeting, or movie theater. Not having a sense of etiquette in these specific locations can ruin the event for others in, surrounding, and outside your group or gathering. Remember, particularly if in a theater, it is very rude to have your device on and/or its light shining. It invades the atmosphere and ambience of these types of locations. It is always best to silence your phone; put it where the device light does not disrupt the sight and pleasure of others.

Group Texts

If you find yourself the recipient of a group text, should you have more to say after your initial general response to the group, it is preferred etiquette to provide a more detailed response text directly to the person originating the text, not via the group's link. It is quite annoying to be on a group text and continue to receive text responses or other conversations in the link once the original text message completed its purpose. So do the polite thing, and change to personal, one-to-one messaging with whomever you wish to speak with once the group information is finalized. In other words, do not respond to the original text message if it is a group text. Respond to the sender or another individual directly.

Responding to Text Messages

If you receive a text message, etiquette says to respond as soon as possible. If you are in a situation where you cannot carry on a correspondence, let the sender know quickly. Say you will get back with them soon. Never leave someone wondering if you received a message. Some kind of response, whether positive or negative, is always proper. It is rude to send or receive a text message and then suddenly disappear off the face of the earth, leaving the conversation confused or unfinished. Of course, it is another matter if your device loses battery. Still, it is not wise to begin a text message without a full battery to carry on a conversation or communication. Not doing so speaks of thoughtlessness or unprofessional preparation.

E-mail and so On

It is important to always make a good impression. And it is no different when it comes to e-mail addresses, Twitter identifications, or Facebook and other social media impressions. Remember that what goes on the internet is always on the internet, even if you delete it. What you put on the worldwide web and how you identify yourself via your e-mail address or social media IDs can be telling. Create these titles and addresses with appropriate and clear language. Do not use suggestive or bad taste in your choices. Make a good impression by having your e-mail or other tech identifications clear and logical to their purposes.

Always follow the rules for the internet, computer, and other technology use. It is always important not to skirt around security barriers, use inappropriate websites, or visit shady chat areas. These practices can give others the wrong impressions about you.

Notes

Chapter 4

Table Manners and Eating Etiquettes

There is more to eating than the food itself. How you eat and the way you behave while eating is just as important as food distribution and consumption. Good table manners let people around you enjoy their meals. Social meal gatherings are probably the most frequently used way to entertain. They allow for interesting food choices and lively conversations around the dinner table. Knowing table manners and social eating etiquettes are importance for their success. You must look elegant while you eat so not to offend or make the experience unpleasant for others. No one likes to see a clumsy, disorderly, or messy eater—someone with bad table manners. Good table manners are also the sign of self-assurance, an important virtue that leads to success. Good manners take the struggle out of social eating and make it easy and enjoyable, whether it's a gathering for drinks and appetizers or a formal dinner party.

Good table manners are a courtesy to others, and successful people have good table manners. Although table manners can be different in different parts of the world, good manners show kindness and respect to people everywhere. Remembering things like disposing of chewing gum before you sit down to eat can make or break a good impression.

After sitting down at the table and waiting for everyone else to sit down, unfold your napkin, and place it in your lap. During dinner, if you need to temporarily leave the table, ask the guest to your immediate left and right to excuse you, fold your napkin and place it on the back of or in your seat.

If you have finished eating, place your knife and fork crosswise on your plate. This indicates to your server or host/hostess that you are finished, and they may remove your plate. Place your napkin to the side of your plate. Never put your napkin in your plate.

Men, if you have a hat on, remove it at the dinner table. Place it under your seat or in a safe, out-of-the-way place. Women, you may keep your hat on, unless it is large and in the way of conversation or causes issues with dinner service. If this is the case, politely remove your hat, and place it out of the way. Place your purse under your seat to keep service and movement areas free from obstructions. You do not want a server tripping over your purse, getting injured or spilling food or drinks on others.

Under most circumstances, it is not polite to slurp your drink or soup. Your mother most likely yelled at you if you slurped anything. But in a few countries, it can be seen as an insult not to do so. To eat without slurping may lead those nearby to assume the dinner is not satisfying. In Japan, the same is true for tea. So make sure to know the rules of etiquette for the country where you plan to travel. It could save you some embarrassment. Nevertheless, here we just focus on common etiquette basics 101.

When at a restaurant, encourage everyone to go ahead and make their drink and food selections before you socialize. Also, make sure to greet your server when he or she comes to your table. Learn and remember the server's name. Refer to the person by name. This shows respect for the wait staff and helps expedite service. Let your guest(s) order first. At the end, encourage your guest(s) to leave a fair tip for the wait staff. If they do not, and there is no reason for not doing so, make sure to cover it. Make sure to let the staff serving know they did a good job. Wait staff should not be punished for your guest's rudeness. On the other hand, if your wait staff did a poor job, reflect that in the tip. If necessary, speak to the manager. He or she needs to know.

General Things to Remember While Eating

1. Dispose of chewing gum before you sit down to eat. Wrap it in a piece of paper and throw it in a trash basket. Never split it out on the ground or place on your dish or under furniture.

2. Chew your food with your mouth closed.

3. Do not talk when you have food in your mouth.

4. Wait to start eating until your hostess has started, or has instructed you to begin.

5. Sit up straight, and help carry on a pleasant conversation.

6. If you use a teaspoon for stirring, put it on a plate or saucer. Never leave a teaspoon in a cup; it can upset the cup.

7. When you have finished your soup or dessert, leave the spoon on a plate.

8. When eating soup, dip the spoon away from you so it will drip over the bowl, not on you lap. Sip without noise from the side of the spoon.

9. When cutting food with a knife, hold your fork in your left hand with the tines down.

10. Break bread into small pieces and butter one piece at a time.

11. When passing your plate to the hostess for a second helping, place the silverware near the center of the plate. Do not take the silverware off and hold it or put it on the table.

12. Always leave the bread and butter spreader on the bread and butter plate. Or if there is not one, on the salad plate.

13. When the meal is over, partly fold your napkin and lay it at the left side of the dessert plate or final dish plate.

14. Do not take the last piece of any food item unless everyone at the table is satisfied first. Ask first. It is rude to take more than your share.

Other Considerations

Some formal dinners include assigned seating arrangements for guests. Place cards with guest names are placed with dinnerware on the table. At sit-down dinners, guests may be seated by alternating genders—man, woman, man, woman, and so on. Sometimes couples are separated to sit between or among other guests. And some hostesses and hosts place couples together at the table. It really is just up to them. One thing is for sure, if you are a guest at a dinner with place cards, it is important that you *do not* take it upon yourself to change the seating arrangements. It is rude. There is usually a good reason for guest placements.

Guests should note it is best not to talk politics or religion at a dinner party. Manners and etiquette call for restraint. This is the rule unless the host or hostess takes the conversation in that direction. Dinner parties are for fun, not debate. There is a time and place for differences of opinion.

There is always a bit of confusion about finger foods versus fork and knife. You may eat the following foods with your fingers: barbecue ribs, small fried chicken pieces or wings, boiled shrimp, carrot sticks, cabbage wedges, turnip strips, olives, radishes, corn on the cob, most raw fruits, small whole pickles, candied fruits, potato chips, breads, cookies, and small finger appetizers. Helpful note: If you are not sure how to eat something watch your hostess or host, and do as they do.

Eating new things can be adventurous. If food is being served that you do not like or have never tried, ask your hostess or host to give you a small serving first. Everyone's taste buds are different. Your tastes can also change from time to time. So when you are uncertain about a food, or if you are willing to try a food you did not like before, just ask for a small taste or bite. This way you are not wasting food you may not like. It is also a way to learn new foods you may enjoy.

Serving a Meal

Successful people also use manners and etiquettes when serving a meal. Here are a few tips to remember.

- Serve and remove dishes from the left. Most people are right-handed and can serve themselves more easily if you hold a dish on their left.
- Serve and remove beverages from the right, so you will not reach in front of someone.
- When you clear the table, first take away the serving dishes, salt and pepper, and bread and relish trays. Then remove the dishes and silverware. Never stack the dishes while at the table. Scrape and stack them as soon as you take them to the kitchen. Never scrape in front of your guests.

- When you are serving more people than can sit comfortably at a table, serve buffet style. The utensils, drinks, and the food are placed on the table in a special way. Guests serve themselves. They may or may not sit at a table.

- For a buffet meal, try to plan food that does not have to be cut with a knife. Precut meats are best for quick service and easy eating.

Setting the Table

When hosting or attending a formal or informal dining event, it is important to know the proper placement of dishes, silverware, and napkins. The table is always set according to the menu and how the way food will be served. Also, the number of guests determines the table setting.

There are different ways to serve. Some dining situations call for guests to eat at the table, their food-filled plates served to them. The hostess, host, or head of the family serves everyone. Other scenarios call for food to be passed around the table in large dishes, and guests serve themselves. Sometimes, guests eat buffet style, which means all the food is put on the table and you serve yourself there, but you sit down to eat in other rooms or outside.

The silverware and dishes that are used to set a table depends on the menu, the way the main dish will be served, and on the occasion—party or just family. You might not use all the dishes and silverware illustrated every day, but you should learn where they should be placed so that when these dishes are at your place, you know how to use them.

When you set a table,

- Place napkins and place mats one inch from the edge of the table. Allow at least twenty to twenty-four inches for each place setting.

- Cups and saucers are set on the right-hand side of plate, alongside the spoons.

- Napkins are left of or underneath the forks. The lower-right-hand corner should be the loose or open corner of the napkin. Basically, it should open like a book.

- Glasses should be in upper-right-hand side of the point of the knife. If iced tea or other glass is used, place at the right of the water glass.

- Silverware should be placed in the order the guest will use it when they eat. Pieces to be used first go on the outside, and pieces to be used last go on the inside, toward the plate.

- Set the knife at right of the plate, with cutting edge toward the plate.

- Forks are set left of plate, tines up. If a knife is not needed, place the forks at the right with the spoons.

- Place spoons at the right of the knife, bowls up.

- Dessert silverware is often served with the dessert course. Place one inch from the edge of the table.
- The salad plate is served with the main course. Place the salad plate left of the forks. If a bread-and-butter plate is not used, place the salad plate in its place or just above the dinner plate.
- The bread-and-butter plate is placed at the upper left-hand side of the main plate. Place the butter spreader on the edge of the plate, parallel to the bottom edge of the table. If you are using the bread-and-butter plate for salad, you can place the butter spreader on the table, right above the dinner plate.

Dining

Using the correct fork, reaching for and taking a drink from the correct glass, or selecting the correct plate for your butter and bread is important. You do not wish to upset the placement and use of silver or dinnerware. A tip or rule of thumb to remember which side is which while sitting at the table, is to raise your hands. Put your right pointer finger and thumb together to form a circle, and extend your other fingers straight out to form a "d." Do the same with your left pointer finger and thumb, and extend the other fingers to form a "b." So visualize the left side is for bread—b. Your right side is for drink—d.

Following are a few examples of dinnerware, glassware, and silverware placements for a variety of dining experiences.

Breakfast Place Setting

Brunch Place Setting

Lunch

Dinner Place Setting

Formal Place Setting

Formal Dining Place Setting with Salad, Soup, and Dessert Placements

List of Placed Items

1. Napkin
2. Salad Fork
3. Dinner Fork
4. Dinner Knife
5. Soup Spoon
6. Teaspoon
7. Butter Knife
8. Bread Plate

9. Dinner Plate
10. Salad Plate
11. Soup Bowl
12. Coffee Cup or Teacup
13. Dessert Plate
14. Water Glass
15. Red Wine Glass
16. White Wine Glass

Table settings include the tablecloth, centerpiece or decorative focal point, dinnerware, glassware, silverware, and napkins. Coordinating the table designs, colors, and style of service is the secret to making the table setting an attractive background for the food and theme of the occasion or event.

Some formal table settings include place cards or seating arrangements. Again, if you are a guest, *do not* change the seating arrangements. To do so is rude. The host/hostess usually has good reasons for the guest placements.

Tea and Receptions

A delightful tradition in entertaining or small gatherings is the tea, or sometimes more modernly referred to as a reception. A tea can be simply social, seasonal, or have a specific purpose. Hosting or attending a tea is a great way to practice a variety of etiquettes.

Some use teas to honor a person or a special occasion. Teas can celebrate events, such as weddings and baby showers, promotions, and graduations. They can celebrate purpose and success. They can be formal or informal; they may have a theme.

It is fun to host or attend a tea. In either case, etiquettes and manners are always observed. Hosting or attending a tea is a great way to practice a variety of etiquettes. Make sure to be informative about or know the purpose and attire expected for guests. Follow the etiquettes suggested in this book to be a success in whichever case you find yourself.

Hosting a Tea

When the tea is small, the beverage and simple foods may be placed on a tray or small table. The beverage served is tea and sometimes coffee or both. A variety of teas are usually offered, as well as regular and decaf coffee. The fare is basic finger foods or appetizers.

A teapot, coffeepot, sugar, and creamer can be arranged to the right of the seated hostess/host for easy serving. Cups and saucers, small stacked plates, silverware, and napkins are placed to host's/hostess's left. Or the items can be set out in a buffet-style service. Small favors are a nice touch for your guests but are not required. The tea and social gathering in itself is your gift to your guests. On another note, if you are attending a tea, it is nice to bring the host/hostess a small gift. You will be sure to get another invite!

Heat Fresh Cold Water
200-210 degrees

After tea brews...
drain tea bag over cup
by wrapping string
around bag tightly...
Remove tea bag and
set aside on saucer

Steep For 3-5 Minutes

Pour 6-8 oz
Heated Water Over
Single Tea Bag

Tea Brewing

Notes

Chapter 5

Important Etiquettes that Promote Business Leaders

It is important to have a current business card; even if only to exchange as a courtesy in introductions or card swaps with people of interest. Make sure your card has clear and readable information about you, what you do, and how to make contact. Giving out your card helps people remember you and makes a personal connection. Taking cards from individuals is a way to remember personal connections and why they are important to you. You should also write facts you gathered from your encounter on the back of your collected card. These are important facts about that individual for possible later meetings or correspondence. Remembering facts about anyone with whom you speak makes your link more personal. It helps you focus and recall why you were interested in that individual. It also makes other people feel you were paying attention to them. It is very flattering to think someone was paying attention to you and the conversation remembered.

Business Cards

Business cards may seem outdated among technology, but in reality, they make interactions more personal. Exchanging business or personal cards makes for good personal contact. Cards also take on a life of their very own. So make yours unique to you. If you receive a card and do not wish to keep it, never toss it at the event where you collected it. That is rude. Dispose of it later, at home or the office. You would not want to see your card left behind or tossed. It shows personal disinterest. Nothing is as tacky as making someone feel he or she is undesirable or not part of your circle or interests.

Greeting Business Leaders

When meeting individuals in a business setting, it is important to exchange business cards, as mentioned previously. Never go to a meeting or business gathering without your cards. They are your linking tools. This is a way to stand out among others during meet and greets.

Next, always look your acquaintance or new associate face-to-face during the greeting, giving them your undivided attention. This is vital to remembering names and pertinent personal information about those you meet. As new individuals enter your greeting circle, introduce your acquaintance or associate to the arrivals to your conversation. Not only is this polite, it helps you remember names and facts too.

Handshakes can never be overrated. It shows good etiquette to extend your hand as you greet and give your name. While doing so, always look the individual in the eye. Focus on what the person says to you. Use a firm grip, but do not over squeeze the hand you shake.

After introductions, exchange your business cards before you move on to groups or individuals not in your immediate greeting circle. Always excuse yourself from the group or individual before moving on to meet others. If leaving an individual, you should ask if he or she would like to mingle or circle forward with you. If they join you, remember to introduce them and yourself to the new group as you enter a situation of introductions.

At the end of the meet and greet phrase of the gathering, if possible, pick an aisle or table end seat so that you can excuse yourself without interrupting the meeting or gathering if you need to leave early or temporarily visit the restroom. Once the meeting begins, silence your phone, stop talking, and give your full attention to those speaking or presenting. If possible, write down keynotes during the meeting. You never know if you will need to use the information in later conversations that will help further your career or current situation. Plus, it is polite to show interest in the speaker. Others around you may be interested too. So do not become a distraction. Afterward, respond appropriately to the conclusion of the speaker's presentation whether by clapping or giving affirmative kudos. If you get a chance to meet the speakers, have something interesting to comment on about their presentations (for example, something from your notes). This is flattering and will show you paid attention, as well as appreciated their efforts.

If you are at a business luncheon where table seating is involved, never exclude someone from sitting at your table if room is available. When looking for a seat, and if you are not alone, never accept a seat at a table where you and your acquaintance or associate cannot sit together. To leave the individual without a seat in the group while you sit is rude. It is courteous to include your acquaintance or associate, or move to a table where both of you can be seated together. Again, when the speakers begin, give them your full attention. Try not to make a lot of noise with plates and silverware while they speak. You can continue to eat and drink if not finished, but do so quietly.

As stated earlier, if you need to temporarily leave the table, place your napkin folded on the back of your seat. If you have finished eating, place your knife and fork crosswise on your plate. This indicates to your server that you are finished, and your plate may be removed. Never put your napkin in your plate.

Notes

Chapter 6

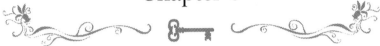

Etiquettes for Academic Success

L et me share just a few words about academic etiquettes. It is always important to show your instructors, teachers, or professors the respect due them. If they have a title, use it. They have earned them, and it shows etiquette and great respect to refer to them by their titles. They will appreciate it.

When a professional gives you a syllabus or set of guidelines, read it fully and follow it completely. If you have questions about it, ask them to clarify. The professional has gone to a lot of trouble to outline the best way to have success in the course. It is simple; do not fight it, and do it the professional's way.

It is important to always turn in your work or assignments on time, if not early. This is a considerate etiquette and worth your time and effort. Make sure to read all written comments your instructor takes the time to share with you on your returned work. Incorporate these tips in your ongoing work to show you consider their input valuable to your success. Because it is!

If you have questions or do not understand a grade or comment, make sure to speak with your instructor directly. Never go behind or above the instructor to inquire about an explanation. If a conference with your instructor is not productive or satisfactory, then you may seek other help with the situation. Just remember to show respect and etiquette by following the proper steps of this academic inquiry process.

In summary, it never hurts to speak with your instructor about the reason behind a given grade. If you are not satisfied with or confused about a score, inquire about the bases for it. Let the instructor know you are interested in correcting your mistakes in order to do better on future assignments.

It is important to arrive to class on time, if not a few minutes early. And unless it is an emergency, never leave early. Make time to have a weekly conference, even if brief, with your instructor to check your ongoing progress. Never wait until it is too late to approach your instructor for help or extra assignments. Checking your progress weekly shows your interest in your success. Waiting until the last minute to ask for help shows poor judgment and lack of concern. Why should your instructor be concerned with helping you to improve your grade if you are not? Your instructor's time is valuable. Do not expect him or her to waste it on your lack of concern. Have forethought and etiquette for your academic success. There is no such thing as luck. Timely preparation equals success.

Notes

Chapter 7

Simple Etiquettes for Social Success

Particular to Boys and Men

Males are fortunate. Even though they have special rules of polite etiquette, they are simple and not hard to remember. The few tips that follow may seem old-fashioned, but they will help every boy develop into a confident and respected man.

- Males stand up promptly whenever a female or older man enters the room, area, or comes over to talk with him. A simple show of respect for others.

- A male opens the door for a female and then steps back to let her enter the doorway first. Courteously allowing entrance before him.

- Males seat females at the table before they sit. They do this in the following manner. The male stands behind the chair and pulls it out far enough for a female to get between it and the table. Then, as the female bends her knees to sit, he pushes the chair gently toward the table, so it will be there for her to sit on.

- Males remain standing at the table until females are seated. In a group, males wait for their dinner partners to be seated before they sit down. When a female approaches a table to talk, males stand and remain standing as long as she is there, unless she indicates for him to sit, which she should do if she plans a lengthy conversation.

- A male opens a car door for a female. He gets into a car after she is settled in the car. And he gets out first so he can open the car door for the female to exit.

- A boy shakes hands each time he is introduced to a man, a boy, or any woman who first offers her hand. Boys should develop a firm but comfortable, brief handshake. Never give a bone or knuckle crusher.

- Always look directly at the person whose hand you are shaking.

- A boy carries packages for his mother or any woman or girl he is walking with.

- A male should help a female remove her coat in a church, theater, or restaurant. At which point, he then either hangs it up, drapes it over a chair, or takes it to a coat check room for her.

- A males should give the order to a server after first asking the female what she would like to eat and drink. If she is not ready to order, he should ask the server to come back in a few minutes.

- A male should remove his hat when he is introduced to someone, when he enters a house, church, a restaurant, and so on.

- A male should give up his seat to a female standing near him on a bus, subway, or train.

- Males should walk on the curbside of the street when with females.

- Males should make sure to wear clothes appropriately so as not to embarrass or offend others. Specifically, males should not wear baggy pants dropped below the buttocks or loose belts. No wife-beater shirts. And, always have a shirt on unless shirtless is appropriate to the event.

Particular to Girls and Women

Despite some people trying to make it a problem, manners and etiquettes really do not have anything to do with being liberated or with women's lib. It is about learning behavior that shows respect of others. Good behavior and etiquettes are not sexist. These few tips will help young girls become confident and respected women:

- Allow males the opportunity to exhibit courteous, respectful behavior and etiquettes. It helps with their self-confidence and with positive male development. If you have sons, male friends, boyfriends, or husbands, it is so important to help develop and then expect them to exhibit respectful behaviors not only to you, but toward others as well. Hold them accountable for etiquette practices. It's not sexist to expect and allow good behavior.
- Be kind—not bossy, boastful, or selfish—in all situations.
- When someone hurts your feelings, accept apologies without reiterating the issue.
- Never whisper to one person in front of others.
- Stand up when you are being introduced to someone your age or older.
- Use people's names when you ask or answer questions.
- Look others in their eyes when being introduced. Remember their names.
- When meeting someone you know, always greet first and then introduce the individual with you.
- If you are greeting someone who may not remember your name, always use your name in the greeting to help with probable awkwardness.
- You might offer your hand for a firm but not overpowering handshake if the situation calls for it.

- Be respectful to those who serve you. Say, "Please," and, "Thank you," when you order or ask for service. Respect their work, and appreciate what they do for you.

- If dining out with a male paying for the dinner, quickly figure out what you want to eat and/or drink and tell him what you wish. Let him place the order with the server.

- If someone else is covering the cost of breakfast, lunch, or dinner, be thoughtful not to be overly expensive with your order. If in doubt of how much to spend on your selection, ask what the other person plans to order. This will give you a budget.

- If dining out with a group, quickly figure out your order so you are ready when it is your turn. Socialize after you know what you plan on ordering.

- If traveling or gathering as a group, offer to help with gas or other expense.

- If a male(s) stands up as you approach a grouping of guests or table of peers, and if you plan to have an extensive conversation, let them know they can be seated. Do not make them stand while you carry on more than a brief exchange.

- Make sure to be aware of the length and neckline of your clothes. Accordingly, make sure to stand, bend, sit, and/or climb stairs appropriately so as not to embarrass or offend others. Be careful not to stand too closely to the edge when on a higher or lower level than others. You do not wish to be embarrassed by accidentally exposing yourself.

- Wear same color undergarments with dark or light clothes. Specifically, wear black undergarments under black clothes, and white or cream under white clothes. This makes a big difference when taking photographs with flash. Specifically, you can see the lighter color undergarments under your darker clothes with camera flash reflection.

- If choosing to wear tights or colored hosiery, make sure to select the predominant color in the outfit for the hosiery or tights color.

- Shoe color, if not a neutral, should be in the predominant color of the outfit or the color in the outfit closest to the shoes. Also, if not neutral, match your purse to the shoe color.

Being a Good Sport

It is good to be a gracious winner and a good loser. You should always sincerely congratulate winners and never show poor sportsmanship by being a sore loser. Winning or losing will not reflect negatively on you, but being immature about either situation will show your true character. Having bad character leads to a poor reputation and does not lead to personal, peer, or professional success.

Being a good sport can mean having empathy, as well as accepting outcomes and circumstances. Whether you win or lose, have success or face temporary failure, communicating positivity is key to professionalism and shows good character. Success comes with these two ideals. Furthermore, if you and another person have a clash or misunderstanding, it is always best to confront it one on one with that person. Be upfront with your feelings. Do not let hurt feelings fester. Get your peace. It is best to clear the air and correct misunderstandings that might stifle positive energy between you and others. And, do not wait long to do so. You cannot control how others respond, but you can control your reactions. Whether just feeling it or actually manifesting it, positivity is always success building.

Tips for Service

Tip according to your wait staff's service. To give a great tip for poor service never helps the wait staff achieves service maturity. Reward a good wait staff with a high percentage tip. Always appreciate good service by giving a good tip.

If you are the wait staff, never ask for a tip, and never ask if the patron wants change. This puts the patron on edge and is rude. Just bring them their correct change and they will leave a tip according to your service.

Notes

Chapter 8

Invitations and RSVPs

At a Social Gathering that Includes Food and Beverages

As a Guest

When invited to a social event, whether you are able to attend the gathering or not, always respond to an invitation in a timely fashion. Whether the host or hostess asks for it or not, always give an RSVP. In the context of social invitations, RSVP is a request for a response from the invited person or people. It is an acronym derived from the French phrase, *Rè'pondez s'il vous plai`t*. It literally means, "Reply if you please," or, "Please reply." Sometimes, a host or hostess will add "Regrets Only." Call and let your host or hostess know your attendance intention based on the RSVP request. Besides showing good manners, it is proper etiquette and the mature thing to do.

Limit acceptance and your RSVP to just the invited. In order words, if the invitation is for you, or you and a partner or guest, do not assume you can bring your children, friends, or pet(s). Do not call and ask to bring anyone or pet other than to whom the invite is extended. The invite will indicate if family, extra friends, and/or pets are included.

On the day of the event, it is important to arrive on time; successful people are *on time*. It is polite to arrive no more than five minutes early and no more than ten minutes late. If for some unforeseen reason you are going to be later than ten minutes, call and let your host or hostess know. They then can decide whether to delay serving dinner or social activity. They must be considerate of your situation, but at the same time, not put out their other guests or let food spoil. If you are late, show up as quickly as possible, and transition quietly into whatever stage the event is in on your arrival. Do not make a big deal about being late. Do not put a spotlight on yourself. The gathering is not about you; it is about the gathering as a whole. Moreover, if you are going to be more than thirty minutes late, depending on the length of the event you are invited to, it might be best to let your host or hostess know that unfortunate events will keep you from attending. This releases the host or hostess from the obligation to accommodate you and allows the event to carry on with their other guests in a timely manner.

As a waiting guest, if food is part of the event, do not help yourself to food or drinks, or partake of the dinner or buffet until the host or hostess indicates it's all right to do so. Because food amounts could be limited, do not take more than your share. It is polite to wait until all have been served before you take second helpings. If food or dessert is left over, wait to be offered a share of it before you take some home. And, only take a small share.

Most times when invited to a social meal—whether it is breakfast, lunch, brunch, or dinner—it is nice to offer the host or hostess a hand in cleaning up immediately after the meal is over. If you are among a group of guests or the only guest, graciously offer your help. Hopefully, if there are other guests, they should take your lead and do so as well. If they do not, you certainly are the responsible one. Even if it is just offering minor assistance, help do some small task with your host or hostess with a pleasant attitude. Think of it as just another way of socializing after your meal. If your host or hostess needs your help, it will be accepted. But if not, take your place among the other guests and socialize or entertain each other while you wait for your host or hostess to return to the gathering. If you are the only guest, stay with your host or hostess as they manage the meal aftermath and carry on a social conversation.

In the end, as a guest, make sure to graciously depart the social event or gathering a few minutes before the time indicated in the invitation. Do not overstay your welcome, and try not to be the last to leave. As you depart, make sure to thank your host or hostess for including you. A thank you note, text, or email is always in good form a few days after you attend a social invitation, but if the event was a formal affair, it is good etiquette to send your host or hostess a thank you note.

On another note, it is nice to bring a gift to the host or hostess of the social event, but it is not mandatory. If you bring a gift, it is usually some small token of friendship, an appetizer, or a bottle of wine. If you bring an appetizer or drink to share at the party or gathering, such as a bottle of wine or other beverages, do not take it home with you. Leave it as a gift. It is most impolite to take it back, even if it was not used or opened at the time. Do take your dish if it is not disposable.

More on Accepting Invitations

Being invited to an event, dinner, party, ceremony, and so on, is socially desirable and, of course, can be fun. There are a few etiquettes to consider when accepting an invitation. Courtesy is of the upmost importance and at the top of the etiquette pyramid. Practice the following.

1. Consider your invitation. Is it something you want to do? Are you available?
2. Answer your invitation immediately, so your host or hostess does not have to wonder if you are attending.
3. Never assume you are the only guest invited; arrive on time.
4. Never extend your invitation to others without permission from the originator of the invitation. They may

have a guest limit or wish to have a certain guest list or purpose in mind. It is rude to show up with uninvited guests (human or animal).

5. If you have houseguests or have arrangements with others pending, decline the invitation. Do not put the host or hostess on the spot to accommodate your situation and your guest. If there is room or if the event warrants more guests, you will likely be asked to bring along your guest. Never assume it is okay.

You as the Host or Hostess

Event planning takes organization. If you choose to cater your party, do it well rather than try something new or over the top. If cooking is not your thing, get help or hire a caterer. Whether you do the catering and decorations yourself or get someone else to do it, you will be more relaxed and in a good mood if you get all the work done in advance. After your preparations, if possible, set aside some quiet self-time before your guests arrive. Have everything ready at least thirty minutes ahead. Some guests may show up early, so be ready. Remember, the objective of entertaining is to enjoy your guests as well as yourself. I read somewhere a cliché of Aristotle that still holds true: "Pleasantest of all ties is the tie of host and guest."

To have successful gatherings, and have your guests continue to come, make your events special. Reflect fun themes in your invitations. Make your events memorable in some way by making them different from the norm.

Sending out invitations for your gathering or event can be informal or formal. In either case, providing details is important. The more details you can provide guests, the more comfortable they will be in accepting your invitation and understanding what is expected of them as guests. Important details should include, but are not limited to, the following.

- Purpose or Theme of the event or gathering
- Date and time
- Location of event
- Host or hostess contact information
- Date by which an RSVP is expected
- Guest attire
- If pertinent, include whether guests are to bring something (for example, gifts, shared foods or appetizers, personal drinks)
- Registered store information if gifts are part of the event/gathering.

Next, plan a menu so that everything can be prepared in advance, and platters can be exchanged and refreshed in the kitchen. It is important for you to enjoy your event as much as your guests. Be aware if any of your guests have food allergies. Have a few foods marked for these individuals. Not only will they appreciate your efforts, it will make them not feel left out as guests. Nothing is worse than being a guest and there is nothing for you to eat or drink.

As the host or hostess, be gracious to your guests, even unexpected ones. If guests show up late, show up uninvited, or if they did not respond affirmatively and are unexpected, be kind. Make them feel welcome despite the mix-up in the invitation dynamics. Move on and have fun.

If you are the host or hostess of a social food event such as breakfast, lunch, brunch, or dinner, you should do as little clean up as possible directly following the meal. The purpose of your social event is to entertain your guests, first, with food and then with more social interaction. If a guest or guests ask to help you clean up, it is perfectly acceptable to take them up on their offer to help you clear the immediate dining area. But only allow a small amount of help from your guests. Remember, they were invited for socializing and entertainment. So after you secure refrigerated items, move yourself and your helpful guests back to the group or gathering for the remaining time set for the event or social activity. After the last guest has departed, you can clean up. If it is late, soak items that need attention, and save the rest for the next morning.

On another note, if a guest brings an appetizer or drink to share at the party or gathering, such as a bottle of wine, it is polite to open it and share it (unless more than enough is already open and available.) If someone brought food to share, make it immediately available to the other guest. Afterward, if the dish is not disposable, it is polite to clean the dish for the guest to take back home. Thank them for sharing.

Notes

Chapter 9

Travel Etiquettes

Successful people tend to travel more than the norm. They seek world knowledge and relaxation through travel. Sometimes just for the fun of travel itself. Sometimes their work calls for them to travel. Manners and social etiquettes will get you a long way when traveling. These concepts help with positive interactions with people you come in contact with during travel. Positive interactions make for better situations while traveling. They effect those involved with you during travel, those in charge of your travel arrangements, and those whom you just happen to come into contact with during your travel. Giving a little attention to manners and social etiquettes helps make your travel positive and successful. Here are a few etiquette tips to make part of your travel routine.

- Successful travelers must have courage to meet the challenges of travel. Along with courage, they must always be polite, kind, and, above all, patient.

- Make sure to have plenty of time. Do not be rushed. Be early. Rushing or being late can cause serious travel mistakes. And, unnecessary stress.

- Do not over pack. Less is better when it comes to carrying or moving your luggage around.

- When flying, wear your heavier clothing items, such as coats, sweaters, and raincoats. This helps keep your suitcase light and gives you something to keep warm with in cold airports and planes.

- The simple rule of thumb is to allow those exiting an area to go first. Then you enter. This applies whether exiting or entering a bus, an airplane, a restroom, an elevator, and a general doorway or entrance area of any kind.

- If riding in an elevator, as it comes to a stop, move to the side walls or step out temporarily, holding your arm across the elevator door to keep it open as others exit. If you are waiting to enter the elevator, remember to let others exit it before you enter.

- If you are near the elevator button panel, ask entering passengers what floor they need. In turn, if you enter the elevator and no one asks you, or if you cannot push the floor buttons, ask the person closest to the panel to push your floor button. And, of course, always say, "Thank you," or, "Excuse me."

- Escalators are important methods of moving people quickly if used appropriately. If you are on an escalator, move your luggage and yourself to the right side. Thus leaving the left side open for people to walk up the escalator around you, which actually gets them to the top much faster than just letting the escalator move them up at its automatic pace. Once at the top of the escalator, move away quickly, so you do not cause others to stumble or bottleneck the exit.

- The above applies to a moving sidewalk conveyor belt too. Walk or stand to the right side to allow others movement around you at a faster pace.

- When reading sidewalk, subway, train, or terminal signs, make sure to move to the side area, out of the center or main walkway, as you make your plans or movement. Never stand in the way. Making others move around you to pass by or through the area is rude. Never stop and stand in the middle of an aisle or walkway.

Shopping Etiquette

When shopping there are a few etiquettes and manners to contemplate. It is important to take your time and have consideration for store staff and other shoppers. Their time is as important as yours. Make sure to give yourself time to shop so that you do not find yourself in a rushed rude frenzy. It is especially important to use your etiquette to be kind and considerate in holiday seasonal shopping scenarios.

Below are suggestions to put into practice that will make your shopping and the experience of others better.

- If you have more than 10 items, DO NOT cue in the limited item checkout line. That cue is for shoppers who have few items and wish a fast checkout.

- Unless you are handicap, do not use a handicap cue or parking space.

- Be kind to those using mobile handicap scooters, shopping carts, buggies, or wheel chairs, etc. These individuals have limited reach and mobility. They cannot move electric carts as well as you can maneuver around them. Give way to them.

- Do not block shopping aisles. Have your cart to one side or the other. Do not park it down the middle of the aisle while you seek out items.

- Do not go through a fast food drive up window if you have a large take out order. A drive up's basic purpose is for fast quick simple service orders. If you have a large order, even if it is a "to go" order, go inside the restaurant to place it.

- Do not go through a pharmacy drive thru line with questions, a questionable prescription, or a large prescription order. Go inside. A drive through is for quick drop offs and pickups.

- Remember, a drive thru or limited item line is for quick service only. Be courteous.

Houseguest Etiquettes

If you host houseguests, make sure their room and bathroom areas are clean and fresh. Set conditioned air sources at an appropriate and comfortable level for the season. Make sure to have a variety of drinks, foods, and snacks. Nothing is worse for guests than being cold, hot, or hungry. Let them know when meals can be expected. Ask if they have allergies you should be concerned about. Check with your guests often to make sure they are settled comfortably and if they need anything. Depending on the length of your guests' stay, make sure to continue to refresh their areas and resupply provisions. If possible, place a small, inexpensive welcome gift in their room.

Sometimes you may be staying as a houseguest while traveling or visiting family or friends. It is important to use etiquette and manners while sharing someone's home. Remember to:

1. If possible, bring a small inexpensive gift of thanks for your hosts. If an occasion occurs, treat your hosts to a breakfast, lunch, or dinner dining experience. It does not have to be expensive to show your appreciation of their hospitality.

2. Clean up after yourself. Depending on your length of stay, offer to help with minor chores. Specifically, help with the chores that effect your stay and lodging area. For example, ask to help with cleaning your room, washing your sheets, taking out your trash, and perhaps with cooking a meal or cleaning the dishes after a meal.

3. Never raid the refrigerator or pantry without permission. If you munch out completely on an item, replace it. Again, depending on the length of your stay, offer to help with the grocery bill. This is particularly important if you have special food needs or allergies.

4. Never change the air-conditioning settings in your guestroom area without asking your hosts first. If you are uncomfortable, let them know to adjust it.

5. Always send a thank you note for their hospitality, and offer an invitation for them to be your guests in the future.

Hotel Etiquettes

It is important to remember there are people cleaning up after you in a hotel, bed and breakfast, and so on. Be kind. Do not trash your hotel room. Clean up any extra mess you might make while staying. Do not leave your mess for the staff to clean. Here are a few things you can do to help make your exit better for the staff:

- Collect and place all your used/dirty washrags and towels in the empty tub or shower.

- Place all your garbage in the trash can. If your garbage does not fit, take it out to a hotel trash receptacle or waste container. Do not place on the floor outside your door.

- When finished with your room service meals, call guest services for it to be picked up. Do not sit it outside on the floor by your door. No one wants to see your left over food or used dishes as they travel the hall.

- Return the air-conditioning level back to normal if you adjusted it. Make sure the water faucets are off, and turn off the lights when you exit. Lock the door, and return your key.

Notes

Chapter 10

Being Part of a Group

When joining a group or team—whether it's a business, social, sports or athletic, fund-raising, or gaming group—it is important to have group etiquette. Group membership usually has privileges, and with privilege comes responsibility. Reliable and successful groups have membership rules, policies, and procedures. These must be adhered to via group etiquettes. To make a group effective, members must follow the rules. Being a good member and following the policies and procedures are important to the group as a whole. It helps make a group or team effective.

Being fair, honest, and responsible is part of group etiquette. Honor is high on the list of a good group member's desired characteristics. Group dynamics can be tricky. So mean what you say, and say what you mean. Below are a few tips to remember as a group or team member.

1. When accepting a group invitation, know the rules, policies, and procedures expected of group members, and follow the rules. Once you join, it is your responsibility to be a good member.

2. When committing to a committee or group activity, never dump them for a better offer. Always follow through with your commitment to the group's purpose until it is complete. Then, if you so desire, change committees or activities. It is extremely rude to leave a group in the middle of your commitment for someone or something better. It shows a lack of etiquette, and even worse, a lack of honor.

3. It is your duty as a good group or team member to always do your best for the group or team's purpose. Offer your expertise when able, and follow through until the group's objective is complete. Be an active and contributing participant.

4. Be a viable part of the group, not a problem for it. The groups' originator or leadership rules. After that, a majority rules. Do not be a troublemaker or sore loser. If you find you do not have the same objectives as the group, leave it once your commitment is complete.

5. Follow the rules of the group, activity, or event.

6. Be a cheerful and productive member of the group. Nothing is worse than being invited to participate in

an event or activity, being counted on to complete a group dynamic, and then deciding at the last minute to change your mind about joining. This leaves the group waiting, hanging, or short on needed participants.

Notes

Chapter 11

Dressing for Success

No matter what occasion or purpose, dressing for success is important. Besides your first verbal communication with someone, they get a first impression from the way you dress. Therefore, it is important to determine your fashion style. And it is important to know how your style fits in with the occasion or purpose of your outing. Determine the dress code for the event before you make an unfortunate bad impression. Remember, the right impression can lead to present and future success. There are several obvious places where you need to follow protocol for successfully making the right impression. Here are a few:

- The workplace. There is no excuse for not knowing the dress code for your job and workplace. Make sure to determine the dress code by checking with at least one of the following sources: human resources, your colleagues, manager, or boss. Know what is acceptable wear for all work occasions.

- When either gender goes to an important event—such as a job interview, college or scholarship interview, or events where you represent a group or committee for a specific cause—always dress to impress. You should wear your "Sunday best." Some do not understand what that phrase means or refers to. To wear your Sunday best means to dress as you would to go to church on a special Sunday morning. It means you dress sharp and crisp. No shorts, T-shirts, mini-dresses, and so forth. No unpressed clothes. No extreme fashion styles. Be tasteful.

- You dress to make a positive impression. Dress appropriate for the occasion or purpose.

- Follow the dress code rules for school, work, sports, or wherever dress code rules are established. Usually they are set for your safety or for the safety of others.

- Pay attention to the dress code for the event you are attending. Do not be embarrassed by showing up in the wrong style, an inappropriate outfit, or nonfunctional wear.

- Makeup is best when at a minimum during the day. Less is best for professional success. Evenings may call for a little heavier application of cosmetics, depending on the type of social or professional event. But still apply in moderation.

Making a great impression is part of achieving success. It starts with hygiene etiquette. An example of this is to always be clean, fresh, and well-groomed when around others. Hygiene etiquette is absolutely mandatory when at work, or attending interviews, professional, and social gatherings or events. It is highly important when traveling on public transportation, such as planes, trains, buses, or group taxis. Be aware of body, breath, and clothes odor in close-quarter situations.

Dress for Consideration

It is important to dress for consideration in certain occasions. Weddings and funerals are on top of the watch out list. Tips for both genders as it applies to attending weddings and funerals are listed below.

- Unless you have been requested to, do not wear white or cream as a guest at a wedding. These colors are reserved for the bride and/or bridal party. Pay attention to if the wedding is casual, semiformal, or formal. Note of whether the wedding is held in the morning, afternoon, or evening. These times of day make a difference on the style of wear and accessories. In example, do not wear evening wear for a morning event.

- During a funeral, memorial service, or wake, it is important to consider those in mourning by wearing modest clothes and styles, muted colors, and somber accessories. This is not the time to be in festive, colorful, or flashy wear.

- Keep makeup to a minimum. Less is better when at funerals, church, or other such events.

Notes

Chapter 12

General Tips for a Variety of Scenarios

As presented in this book, etiquettes refer to conventional rules and the application of its manners. Always follow understood and posted rules of conduct, expected behaviors, protocols, or decorum. Observance of etiquettes and manners govern polite and successful people and society. Part of success is to be a lifelong learner of formal etiquettes because successful people constantly refine their senses of decorum. Constantly review this book for reminders and insights into your etiquette growth.

Simple Things to Remember

- First impressions are very important. Personal hygiene is vital to that first impression. Take care of your teeth, nails, hair, and body cleanliness and odor.

- Keep a classic fashion sense and style. Classic is always in fashion.

- Always wear what is event appropriate.

- Be on time for appointments, events, or gatherings. Everyone's time matters and is valuable.

- Do not text and drive. No reason is good enough to endanger your life or the lives of others. Pull over to text someone if you will be unavoidably late or to answer an important question. Otherwise, texting can wait.

- Do not drink and drive. Call a cab if necessary.

- During greetings and introductions, take the pressure off those who may not remember your name by simply reintroducing yourself in the greeting or handshake. To help you remember names, try to repeat, reintroduce, and use names a few times in conversation. Repetition can help your memory and theirs.

- If you do not remember someone's name, it is always best to simply be honest about it. Express that you are sorry, but his or her name has slipped your memory. Make it a point to remember it next time. Use it several times in the conversation.

- If in a public place—whether in a checkout line at the grocery store, post office, a bank, a fast-food restaurant queue, and so on—do not talk on your cell phone. If phone use is important or an emergency, make sure to speak softly, so everyone around you will not know your business. Maybe even step out of line if you cannot get off the phone promptly.

- When shopping, do not leave your basket in the middle of the aisle. It is rude to take up more than your space or to block the aisle.
- When walking a pet, whether on a sidewalk, street, or grassy area, always pick up after it and dispose of waste properly. No one likes to step in pet poop!
- Have your pet on a leash, and control your pet in public areas. This protects your pet and well as others.
- If you are sharing a walking path, make sure to keep to one side. Do not block the path; never take over the whole path. It should be easy for others to pass by you.
- Never pause or stop in the middle of a path. Always step to the side … even if momentarily.
- If sharing a path while on a bicycle, give way to pedestrians. Sound your bicycle bell or horn as you approach them to warn you are heading their way.
- In all scenarios, always wait your turn.
- Do not take up more than one parking space.
- Never take a parking spot that someone else is patiently waiting to use. This is extremely rude. If you should do so by accident and you have a chance, explain and make it a point to ask the other person if they'd like you to move.

- Unless you have an appropriate permit, never park in a handicap space. No excuse.
- Never park blocking a driveway or entrance. Park only where approved parking is designated.
- Know your state's driving laws. And when in another state, do not assume the laws are the same. Read, know, and abide by all road rules.
- When invited to a small or large social gathering, event, or dinner, give your attendance response promptly.
- A general rule is not to smoke or vape unless in an approved posted area. Always ask for permission. Never assume it is okay.
- Never attend an event or gathering when ill. Be considerate of other people's health.
- If you need to sneeze, do so into your raised elbow or tissue. This protects your hands for and from handshakes.
- Do not interrupt others when they are speaking. If you have something to say in regard to their conversation, wait for a break in the conversation to give your view or make a point. Do not highjack their conversation to insert your similar story.
- If an agreement or understanding cannot be reached, agree to disagree, and move on to a different topic.
- Even if someone's advice is not useful or warranted, remember to give thanks for help. Advice is knowledge.

It never hurts to take in all advice or options. You can decide later what is useful to your situation.

- No matter their age, speak to everyone with respect and consideration.

Notes

Conclusion

Having manners and using good etiquette is part of a strong foundation that makes a successful person. Just as important, success comes to those who strive to be trustworthy, loyal, helpful, friendly, courteous, kind, obedient to authority, cheerful, thrifty, courageous, clean, and reverent. Therefore, know yourself. Improve yourself. Be the best self you can be. Success does not come by accident, nor by luck. It comes with self-preparation. In short, prepare yourself for a successful future. Use your manners. Learn and apply proper etiquettes. Be mentally awake, and use your moral compass.

Hopefully, this book of manners and etiquettes will help you grow into your better-mannered self, one of respectfulness of others, personal confidence, and peer respect. It is just the start. Make it your mission to continue lifelong etiquette learning. We are never too old to learn something new. And we are never too old to be what we want to be. Be inspired to make good manners and proper etiquettes your foundation for a successful and thoughtful life. Keep this book handy and refresh your behaviors from time to time. And then pass on the knowledge! Your world will be a better place if you do.

Notes

Bibliography

A Handbook of Training for Citizenship through Scouting, 6th ed. New Brunswick, NJ: National Council Boy Scouts of America, 1965.

Better Homes and Gardens. *New Cookbook*. Des Moines, IA: Meredith Corporation, 1978.

Bridges, John, and Curtis Bryan. *50 Things Every Gentleman Should Know*, revised and expanded. Nashville: Thomas Nelson, Inc., 2006.

"Etiquette." *Merriam-Webster.com*. https://www.merriam-webster.com (accessed May 2016).

Junior Girl Scout Handbook, 9th ed. New York: Girl Scouts of the United States of America, 1967.

"Manners." *Merriam-Webster.com*. https://www.merriam-webster.com (accessed May 2016).

The Emperor's Club. Michael Hoffman, director. Universal Studios, DVD, 2003.

About the Author

Jackie Whitehead, EdD, is a native of Alabama and lives in the small coastal town of Orange Beach. Dr. Whitehead is an adjunct lecturer with a concentration in secondary and collegiate education. Dr. J., as she is fondly referred to, received her doctorate in educational leadership,  K–12 and an educational specialist degree, K–12 from Jones International University, Colorado. She received her master of science degree in secondary education with an area of specialization in English language arts from Spring Hill College, Alabama, and a bachelor of science degree in secondary education with a focus in English language arts and business administration from the University of Mobile, Alabama. She currently enjoys guest lecturing on the benefits of etiquettes and manners as a tool for success. Dr. Whitehead's collegiate focus is in the introduction to public speaking, and her secondary education concentrations are drama, English, speech, and business Administration.

Dr. Whitehead has been affiliated with the following professional organizations: American Education Research Association (AERA), the Education Theatre Association (EdTA), and the International Thespian Society (ITS). Whitehead has served as the USTA Southern Section State Community Tennis coordinator (Alabama); the Southern Alabama Tennis Association's executive director, and as the executive director of past Model Expo Events (Mobile, Alabama). She has volunteered as a district judge (Alabama) for the Trumabauer (Theater Arts) Festival and chaired the Bay Area Thespian Shakespeare Competition for many years.

Dr. Whitehead enjoys writing books, articles, plays, producing plays and judging fine arts events and competitions. She also enjoys guest speaking on topics of her expertise and interests and working with youth projects in her community. She enjoys world travel and is a curator for historical masters fine art.

the United States
asters